The Cycle of Fifths

by Emile and Laura De Cosmo

CONTENTS

ISBN 978-0-634-07939-9

7777 W. BLUEMOUND RD. P.O. BOX 13819 MILWAUKEE, WI 53213

In Australia Contact:
Hal Leonard Australia Pty. Ltd.
22 Taunton Drive P.O. Box 5130
Cheltenham East, 3192 Victoria, Australia
Email: ausadmin@halleonard.com

Visit Hal Leonard Online at
www.halleonard.com

About the Authors

Emile De Cosmo has been active as a teacher, musician, and jazz clinician for over 30 years. Playing woodwind instruments, he has freelanced in the New York area with many noted musicians on television, radio commercials, movie soundtracks, club dates, concerts, and shows.

He is formerly an adjunct professor of jazz improvisation at New Jersey City University, an applied music instructor at New Jersey City University and Fairleigh Dickinson University, and concert/marching/jazz band director at Fort Lee High School, and, along with his wife Laura, feature writers for *Saxophone Journal* and *Jazz Player* magazine. He currently is teaching and writing in St. Petersburg, Florida.

He is the author and publisher of the *Polytonal Rhythm Series*, a 19-book collection that has been endorsed by Paquito D'Rivera, Jamey Aebersold, Denis De Blasio, Slide Hampton, John Faddis, Clem De Rosa, Clark Terry, Bill Watrous, *Friday the 13th* film composer Harry Manfredini, Pat LaBarbara, symphony conductor Gerard Schwartz, Bucky Pizzarelli, Eddy Bert, Dizzy Gillespie, Ray Copeland, Leon Russianoff, and many other professionals.

His performance and recording credits include Sarah Vaughn, Dizzy Gillespie, Dinah Washington, Joe Farrell, Vic Damone, Milt Hinton, Slide Hampton, Bucky Pizzarelli, Gregory Hines, Pepper Adams, Terry Gibbs, Sonny Stitt, Four Tops, and many more.

Laura De Cosmo is an active teacher and professional musician who has worked in the New Jersey and New York metropolitan area playing flute, saxophone, clarinet, and singing. She has experience playing in big band, small group, and orchestra. Currently, she is teaching, playing, and writing in St. Petersburg, Florida.

Laura and her husband Emile comprise *The Opposite Sax*, a jazz group performing locally in St. Petersburg, Florida. Along with their recent Hal Leonard publications of *The Woodshedding Source Book* and *The Path to Improvisation*, they also write a weekly jazz column for *The Neightborhood News*.

Preface

Just as gravity acts as a force upon the earth, there is an analogous "force" that acts upon any chromatic tone. This force compels one note toward another that occurs one fifth below the original note (i.e., the fundamental C note resolving down one fifth to the fundamental F note). This natural tendency, which exists in all styles of music, can be described as a continuous spiral of descending, endlessly falling fifths. It is this cyclical progression of notes, tones, or chords that is defined by and depicted in the "cycle of fifths."

Music's primary progression, the cycle of fifths, is also the most crucial for the musician to hear, play, and put into practice. While it is often employed as a means for identifying key signatures, the primary function of the cycle of fifths is to explain the relationships between chords and the natural movement between them. But perhaps even most importantly, the cycle of fifths is the key to understanding the most common cadential progression in music: that of the dominant seventh chord (the chord built upon the fifth step of the major or minor scale) moving to the tonic chord (the chord built upon the first step of the major or minor scale), which in all keys is C7, F7, B♭7, E♭7, A♭7, D♭7, F♯7, B7, E7, A7, D7, and G7.

The fact that the strongest pull in music is the dominant chord to its tonic cannot be emphasized enough, for this relationship holds the key to our understanding of the harmonic movement, or delay, of all progressions in all types of music. Therefore, mastery of the dominant seventh chord and the cycle of fifths progression are vital to the education of the serious music student—no matter what area of music the student's primary interest may be in.

The method used in *The Cycle of Fifths* is actually fun to practice! Each dominant seventh chord is written in the order dictated by the cycle of fifths. Each section featuring a different dominant seventh chord profiles the chord by way of several different rhythms. Playing each dominant seventh chord with different rhythms not only increases the student's fluency in executing each chord, but also takes the boredom out of practicing the exercises over and over in the same way. After playing only a few of the rhythmic exercises found within, the student will notice an immediate increase in the speed with which he or she can play each new exercise. In addition, students of traditional music will have increased their technique and sight-reading ability; students of jazz will have increased their ability to improvise over dominant seventh chords.

Laura and Emile De Cosmo

Introduction

Understanding the strongest "pull" in music—from a dominant chord to its tonic chord—is the doorway to understanding the harmonic movement, or delay, of resolution to the tonic for all progressions in all musical styles. It is this delay of resolution to the tonic that creates the interesting forward motion of music. When resolution to the tonic is effected, the motion comes to rest, and the piece is heard as having reached its ending.

Dominant (V7) to Tonic (17) Chords in Every Key

When we accept the fact that the roots of chords are attracted to roots of chords a fifth lower, then we can better analyze how other chord progressions in music are produced.

- The C dominant chord (C7) gravitates to its tonic: the F chord
- The F dominant chord (F7) gravitates to its tonic: the B♭ chord
- The B♭ dominant chord (B♭7) gravitates to its tonic: the E♭ chord
- The E♭ dominant chord (E♭7) gravitates to its tonic: the A♭ chord
- The A♭ dominant chord (A♭7) gravitates to its tonic: the D♭ chord
- The D♭ dominant chord (D♭7) gravitates to its tonic: the G♭ chord
  (The G♭7 chord spelled enharmonically becomes an F♯ chord)
- The F♯ dominant chord (F♯7) gravitates to its tonic: the B chord
- The B dominant chord (B7) gravitates to its tonic: the E chord
- The E dominant chord (E7) gravitates to its tonic: the A chord
- The A dominant chord (A7) gravitates to its tonic: the D chord
- The D dominant chord (D7) gravitates to its tonic: the G chord
- The G dominant chord (G7) gravitates to its tonic: the C chord

Using the magnetism of the cycle of fifths, we can create chord progressions of all diatonic keys—major and minor. For example, in the key of C major—Cmaj7 to Fmaj7 to Bm7♭5 to Em7 to Am7 to Dm7 to G7 to Cmaj7)—and in the key of C minor—Cm(maj7) to Fm7 to B°7 to E♭maj7♯5 to A♭maj7 to Dm7♭5 to G7 to Cm(maj7).

Confusion of "The Cycle of Fifths" Nomenclature

There are a number of cycle-of-fifths-like terms frequently used by educators, musicians, and students that are misnomers. For example, the cycle of fifths is often called the "circle of fourths," or the "spiral of fourths"—both of which are incorrect. In fact, I once read an article in a newspaper about a musical group called The Circle of Fourths. The group's guitarist, Joe Lynch, stated, "The band's name was derived from music theory; the circle of fourths is based on a progression of harmonies." This perpetual confusion of terms results from thinking in intervals instead of harmonic function. Let the fact be made clear here and now that when an interval of a fourth is inverted it does become an interval of a fifth, and when an interval of a fifth is inverted it does become an interval of a fourth; but the harmonic function V to I remains the same, thus the correct term is "the cycle of fifths."

No matter in which direction the V7 moves—whether *down a fifth* to its tonic (I) or *up a fourth* to its tonic (I), it is still the V7 chord moving to the tonic (I) chord. Any fifth degree of any scale always retains its gravitational V-to-I relation to its tonic and will always fall or move to its tonic when coming to a conclusion. The interval changes in accordance with the direction of the flow, but the harmonic relationship is still V to I.

Other Terms for "The Cycle of Fifths" as Used by Music Theorists

In addition, many alternate terms are used by music theorists for the cycle of fifths. The following is a partial list of these various terms, which may be to blame for the frequent communication breakdowns that often occur in musical discourses:

- Cycle of fifths (correct term)
- Circle of fifths
- Spiral of fifths
- Fifth falls
- Root movement
- Root progressions
- Harmonic progressions
- Dominant cycle
- Circle of chords
- Laboratory progressions
- Functional harmony
- Authentic cadence
- Enchained dominant harmonies
- First-class chords
- Regular resolution

The Overtone Series: Source for the Cycle of Fifths

The phenomena manifested by the gravity of music are many and interrelated. Principally important is the understanding that when an instrument produces a musical tone as the consequence of a vibration in parts of a column of air (as with a trumpet) or a string (as with a guitar), the tones produced, heard as a single pitch, are actually physical combinations of a fundamental tone in conjunction with upper harmonics (partials) or overtones. This *fundamental*—the most prominent tone heard by the human ear—is produced by the longest and, therefore, most slowly vibrating portion of the column of air or string. The upper partials—higher in pitch than the fundamental tones— are then secondarily audible in comparison with the fundamental tone. These parts, the fundamental and its overtones (there are considered to be six principal overtones, but as many as sixteen, twenty-two, and beyond have been reported), naturally assume relative positions represented by what is referred to as the *overtone series*. The fundamental and its overtones produce an altered dominant seventh chord containing tensions extending to the diminished or flatted fifth, augmented fifth, ninth, augmented eleventh, and thirteenth.

The fundamental and its subsequent overtones create a magnetic or gravitational force that puts the fundamental in motion, causing it to resolve, or fall, to another fundamental a fifth below, resulting in the cadential flow of the cycle of fifths. The overtone series from the fundamental tone is as follows:

- C triad = C, E, G
- C seventh chord = C, E, G, B♭
- C ninth chord = C, E, G, B♭, D
- C thirteenth + augmented eleventh chord = C, E, G, B♭, D, F♯, A
- G minor sixth chord = G, B♭, D, E
- E half diminished, or E minor seventh flat five = E, G, B♭ D
- A tetrachord from the C whole tone scale = C, D, E, F♯
- G melodic minor scale ascending = G, A, B♭, C, D, E, F♯, G
- C overtone scale = C, D, E, F♯, G, A, B♭, C
- D major tetrachord = D, E, F♯, G
- D seventh chord = D, F♯, A, C
- D Mixolydian mode = D, E, F♯, G, A, B, C, D
- D ninth chord = D, F♯, A, C, E
- D thirteenth chord = D, F♯, A, C, E, G, B
- E minor tetrachord = E, F♯, G, A
- F♯ half diminished seventh chord = F♯, A, C, E
- G pentatonic blues scale = G, A, B♭, B, D, E, G
- One-third of the chromatic scale from A = A, B♭, B, C
- Two tritones = C to F♯ and E to B♭

Each new fundamental tone produces a new set of theoretical information.

The Tritone

The *tritone*, an interval of an augmented fourth, was called the *diabolus* or the "devil's interval" during the Middle Ages and was avoided melodically. But when used harmonically, it is the most powerful force of harmonic action within the musical universe. The augmented fourth creates a tremendous need for resolution, and should perhaps be more appropriately regarded as the "angel of resolution." The tritone provides the most distinctive characteristic of the dominant seventh chord: tension and unrest, which increases the tonal magnetism and causes a greater need for resolution.

Although tritones were generally avoided in traditional music, the momentum produced by its strong harmonic motion within the cycle of fifths was considered powerful enough to justify its use between IV and vii in the bass of major and minor keys. The chord progression stays in the same tonal center when going from IV7 to vii7 in all tonal centers or keys.

A demand for resolution of overtones as chords or clusters to a fifth below sets up new overtones that also demand resolution.

Learning Musical Theories

During a child's early years, when he or she starts learning and using the native language, constant use of that language refines the child's ability to speak words and sentences. Even through normal daily conversation, one must study one's language in order to master correct grammar. It is said that when learning a new word, the best way for it to become an ingrained part of your vocabulary is to use the new word as many times in conversation and when writing as possible. And so it is with music! When learning new musical theories, a student must also commit them to memory in order to have the greatest mastery over them. For example, a student learning cycle progressions must not only commit those progressions to memory, but learn their every "dialect" or key, in order to be able to "spell" all dominant seventh chords in the cycle of fifths. This is true for students of both performance and composition—the performer must be able to execute the progressions chordally, modally, and melodically; the composer must be able to incorporate and arrange progressions fluently.

An example of the importance of the cycle of fifths can be found in a song composed by jazz great Thelonious Monk called "Skippy," which features the "I Got Rhythm" AABA form, but substitutes and uses sixty-two dominant seventh chords as a progression. The dominant seventh chords move harmonically through the cycle of fifths, as well as chromatically. "Skippy" contains only one tonic chord, which appears in the final measure as the final chord of the piece.

Today, as in the past, jazz educators instruct students to reproduce everything they play on their instruments chromatically—an instruction that is usually ignored because of its difficulty. This practice came about in part because most educators are either pianists, instrumentalists with piano skills, composers, or theorists, and in part because the piano's keyboard, which is arranged chromatically, provides a means of visualization that makes chromatic reproduction easier. But chromatic progressions are an outgrowth of the cycle of fifths; they should actually be learned after one has immersed oneself in both the cycle of fifths and the diatonic cycle of fifths and all its dialects.

In all major keys, the dominant seventh chord built upon the fifth degree of the major scale is a V7 chord. Therefore, upon seeing a dominant seventh chord, a student when improvising should—and must—immediately recognize the key from which it is derived (five steps lower than the root of the V7 chord). For example, C7 = V7 of key of the moment = F major. The following is a list of the twelve V7, or dominant, seventh chords and their respective tonal centers:

- When a C7 occurs, improvise in the key of the F major tonal center
- When an F7 occurs, improvise in the key of the B♭ major tonal center
- When a B♭7 occurs, improvise in the key of the E♭ major tonal center
- When an E♭7 occurs, improvise in the key of the A♭ major tonal center
- When an A♭7 occurs, improvise in the key of the D♭ major tonal center
- When a D♭7 occurs, improvise in the key of the G♭ major tonal center
- When an F#7 occurs, improvise in the key of the B major tonal center
- When a B7 occurs, improvise in the key of the E major tonal center
- When an E7 occurs, improvise in the key of the A major tonal center
- When an A7 occurs, improvise in the key of the D major tonal center
- When a D7 occurs, improvise in the key of the G major tonal center
- When a G7 occurs, improvise in the key of the C major tonal center

If a dominant seventh chord occurs as a V7 chord in a minor key, the student should then improvise in the key of the minor tonal center. For example, if a C7 appears as a V7 chord in the key of F minor, and the C7 chord precedes an F minor chord, the student should then improvise in the key of F minor.

When a student practices the cycle of fifths in each of the twelve tonal centers, they will be able to hear and react more easily to dominant seventh chord changes and express more of what is imagined to be quicker ear/instrument response—whether reading music or improvising.

Although it is important to learn the cycle of fifths in all keys or dialects, it is imperative for today's novice composer or improviser to become familiar with the jazz literature that makes use of the cycle of fifths. If the student learns, analyzes, and memorizes these melodies, improvising on tunes that use cycle changes will become easier.

The following is a list of standard, popular, and jazz tunes containing cycle of fifths changes. Cycle of fifths changes are usually found in the bridge or B section of many AABA tunes, and many tunes begin with cycle changes.

- "After You've Gone" – Creamer/Layton
- "All Blues" – Miles Davis
- "All of Me" – S. Simons/ G. Marks
- "Anthropology" – C. Parker/D. Gillespie
- "Blue Room" – Rodgers/Hart
- "Blue Monk" – Thelonious Monk
- "Broadway" – Wood/McCrae/Bird
- "Celebrity" – Charlie Parker
- "Chasin' the Bird" – Charlie Parker
- "Country Roads" – Steve Swallow
- "Crazy Rhythm" – Caesar/Kahn
- "Dansero" – Hayman/Daniels/Parker
- "Dewey Square" – Charlie Parker
- "Dig" – Miles Davis
- "Don't Get Around Much Anymore" – Duke Ellington
- "Doxy" – Sonny Rollins
- "Exactly Like You" – J. McHugh
- "Four Brothers" – Jimmy Guiffre
- "Freddy Freeloader" – Miles Davis
- "Get Me to the Church on Time" – Lerner/Loewe
- "Honeysuckle Rose" – Fats Waller
- "I Can't Believe That You're in Love with Me" – McHugh/Gaskill
- "I've Got It Bad and That Ain't Good" – Duke Ellington
- "I've Got Rhythm" – George Gershwin
- "I've Got a Right to Sing the Blues" – Arlen/Koehler
- "In a Mellow Tone" – Duke Ellington
- "Jordu" – Duke Jordon
- "Killer Joe" – Benny Golson

- "Kim" – Charlie Parker
- "Lazy River" – Hoagy Carmichael
- "Leap Frog" – Charlie Parker
- "Lil' Darlin'" – Neil Hefti
- "Loads of Love" – Richard Rodgers
- "Lulu's Back in Town" – H. Warren
- "Misterioso" – Thelonious Monk
- "Moody's Got Rhythm" – James Moody
- "Moose the Mooche" – Charlie Parker
- "Perdido" – J. Tizol
- "Scrapple from the Apple" – Charlie Parker
- "Sermonette" – Cannonball Adderley
- "Sister Sadie" – Horace Silver
- "Skippy" – Thelonious Monk
- "Spanish Flea" – Julius Wechter
- "Spinning Wheel" – D.C. Thomas
- "Straight Life" – Freddie Hubbard
- "Sweet Georgia Brown" – Bernie/Pinkard
- "The Preacher" – Horace Silver
- "Watermelon Man" – Herbie Hancock
- "Well You Needn't" – Thelonious Monk

It would take an insurmountable number of pages to list all the songs that feature cycle progressions, which have been by composers renowned and unknown alike. Consequently, we would also have to list all composed music since the tempered scale came into use, which was first suggested by Chinese prince Tsai-yu in 1596—over 400 years ago!

As can be implied by the length of the mere partial list of songs listed above, a jazz player can acquire an abundance of jazz language and style simply by learning melodies. These tunes, as melodic information stored in the mind's ear, become part of the tonal vocabulary to be incorporated—either in bits or at length—when improvising. For every one of the hundreds, if not thousands, of tunes the astute jazz musician has memorized, they have as many ways in which to incorporate the whole or parts of those songs over endless chord changes. This process, over time, occurs automatically.

Therefore, the novice player should begin to memorize as many different jazz tunes as possible in order to expand his or her improvisational fluency and acquire a jazz vocabulary and language—both of which should be continuing processes. After memorizing some of the jazz tunes listed above, the student should first transpose portions, and then eventually complete tunes, into as many different keys as possible (in the order depicted in the cycle of fifths) so as to expand his or her jazz vocabulary even further.

When studying classical harmony, many high school and even college students have difficulty learning the V7-to-I relationship and how strongly it relates to other chord sequences. For such students, memorizing and practicing the cycle of fifths will greatly improve the understanding of this chain of dominants and its relation to the progression, or movement, of chords. And for all students of jazz improvisation, music theory, or composition, learning the cycle of fifths is critical to their mastering their craft.

How to Use This Book

This book is designed to be played as one would read a novel or textbook. Read through a number of pages and mark the place where you decide to stop. In your next practice session, continue where you left off; continue in this way until the book is completed. This book can be played again many times, thus bringing about results that would otherwise take many years of playing experience to accomplish. Depending on their students' needs, teachers may assign lessons from the various sections as they see fit.

Rhythmic Variation

This book incorporates a number of different rhythms. The variations suggest different possibilities in the rhythmic flow of improvisation and break the monotony of playing ordinary exercises. Playing exercises that are both melodic and rhythmic will refine technique, lead to better sight-reading, and improve playing immediately.

Using a Metronome

In order to maintain rhythmic accuracy and to develop a natural sense of meter, the student should use a metronome when practicing these studies.

Accidentals vs. Key Signatures

Accidentals are employed throughout this book rather than key signatures for the purpose of reading ease and to help the student commit the key signatures to memory.

The Goal of Playing the Exercises.

Students should play the exercises in the complete range of their respective instruments with the goal of developing the ability to execute these studies anywhere on an instrument. Also, the student should learn to recognize chordal changes by the sounds of the twenty-four dialects or tonal centers. Accomplishing these things will result in enhanced tone recognition, sight-reading ability, and improvisational fluency.

Exercise 1

Exercise 2

Exercise 3

Exercise 4

Exercise 5

Exercise 6

Exercise 7

Exercise 8

Exercise 9

Exercise 13

Exercise 14

Exercise 17

Exercise 18

Exercise 22

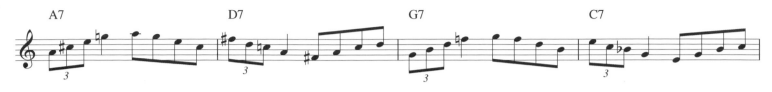

Exercise 23

Exercise 24

Exercise 28

Exercise 29

Exercise 30

Exercise 31

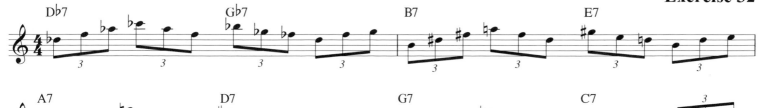

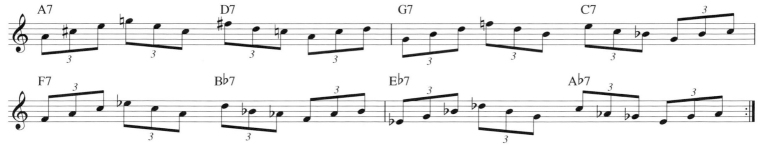

Exercise 36

Exercise 37

Exercise 38

Exercise 42

Exercise 43

Exercise 44

Exercise 45

Exercise 46

Exercise 47

Exercise 48

Exercise 49

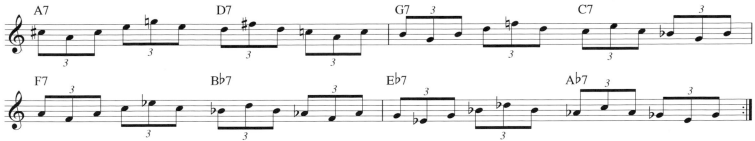

Exercise 50

Exercise 51

Exercise 52

Exercise 56

Exercise 57

Exercise 58

Exercise 59

Exercise 60

Exercise 61

Exercise 62

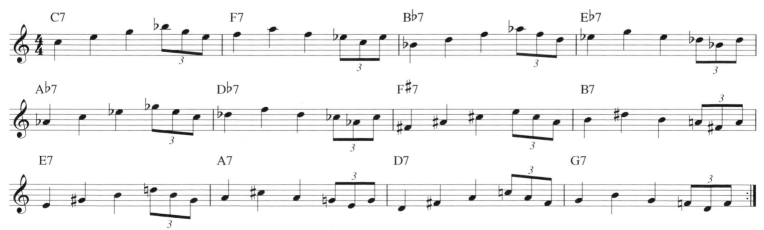

Exercise 63

Exercise 64

Exercise 65

Exercise 69

Exercise 70

Exercise 71

Exercise 72

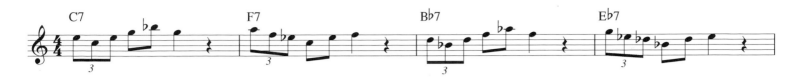

Exercise 76

Exercise 77

Exercise 78

Exercise 83

Exercise 84

Exercise 85

Exercise 89

Exercise 90

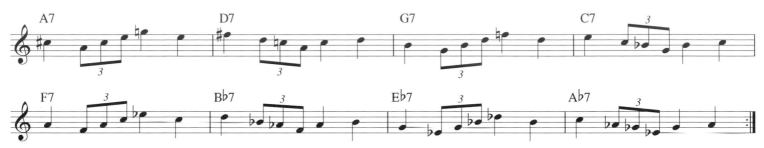

Exercise 91

Exercise 92

Exercise 93

Exercise 94

Exercise 95

Exercise 96

Exercise 97

Exercise 98

Exercise 99

Exercise 100

Exercise 101

Exercise 102

Exercise 108

Exercise 109

Exercise 110

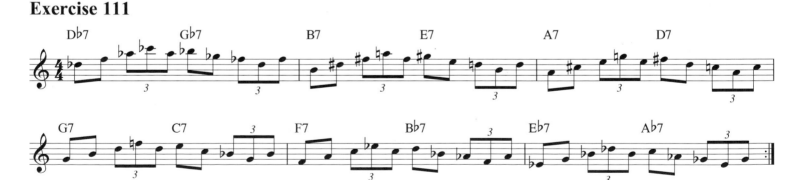

Exercise 111

Exercise 112

Exercise 113

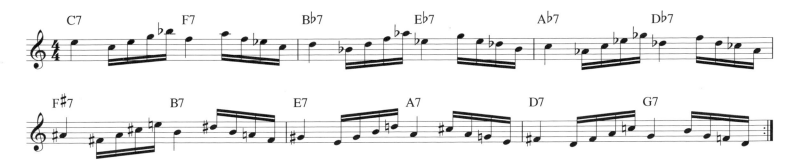

Exercise 114

Exercise 115

Exercise 116

Exercise 117

Exercise 118

Exercise 119

Exercise 120

Exercise 121

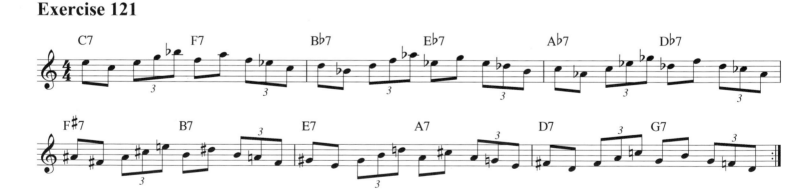

Exercise 122

Exercise 128

Exercise 129

Exercise 130

Exercise 131

Exercise 132

Exercise 138

Exercise 139

Exercise 140

Exercise 141

Exercise 142

Exercise 148

Exercise 149

Exercise 150

Exercise 151

Exercise 152

Exercise 153

Exercise 154

Exercise 155

Exercise 156

Exercise 157

Exercise 158

Exercise 159

Exercise 160

Exercise 161

Exercise 162

Exercise 163

Exercise 164

Exercise 165

Exercise 166

Exercise 167

Exercise 168

Exercise 169

Exercise 170

Exercise 171

Exercise 172

Exercise 177

Exercise 178

Exercise 179

Exercise 180

Exercise 181

Exercise 182

Exercise 183

Exercise 184

Exercise 185

Exercise 186

Exercise 187

Exercise 188

60

Exercise 189

Exercise 190

Exercisc 191

Exercise 192

Exercise 193

Exercise 194

Exercise 195

Exercise 196

Exercise 197

Exercise 198

Exercise 199

Exercise 200

Exercise 201

Exercise 202

Exercise 203

Exercise 204

Exercise 209

Exercise 210

Exercise 211

Exercise 212

Exercise 213

Exercise 214

Exercise 215

Exercise 216

Exercise 217

Exercise 218

Exercise 219

Exercise 220

Exercise 225

Exercise 226

Exercise 227

Exercise 228

Exercise 233

Exercise 234

Exercise 235

Exercise 236

Exercise 241

Exercise 242

Exercise 243

Exercise 244

Exercise 245

Exercise 246

Exercise 247

Exercise 248

Exercise 249

Exercise 250

Exercise 251

Exercise 252

Exercise 257

Exercise 258

Exercise 259

Exercise 260

Exercise 265

Exercise 266

Exercise 267

Exercise 268

Exercise 269

Exercise 270

Exercise 271

Exercise 272

Exercise 273

Exercise 274

Exercise 275

Exercise 276

Exercise 277

Exercise 278

Exercise 279

Exercise 280

Exercise 281

Exercise 282

Exercise 283

Exercise 284

Exercise 286

Exercise 287

Exercise 288

Exercise 289

Exercise 290

Exercise 291

Exercise 292

Exercise 293

Exercise 294

Exercise 295

Exercise 296

Exercise 297

Exercise 298

Exercise 299

Exercise 300

Exercise 301

Exercise 302

Excrcise 303

Exercise 304

Exercise 305

Exercise 306

Exercise 307

Exercise 308

Exercise 309

Exercise 310

Exercise 311

Exercise 312

Exercise 313

Exercise 314

Exercise 315

Exercise 316

Exercise 317

Exercise 318

Exercise 319

Exercise 320

Exercise 321

Exercise 322

Exercise 323

Exercise 324

Exercise 325

Exercise 326

Exercise 327

Exercise 328

Exercise 329

Exercise 330

Exercise 331

Exercise 332

Exercise 337

Exercise 338

Exercise 339

Exercise 340

Exercise 345

Exercise 346

Exercise 347

Exercise 348

Exercise 353

Exercise 354

Exercise 355

Exercise 356

Exercise 361

Exercise 362

Exercise 363

Exercise 364

Exercise 365

Exercise 366

Exercise 367

Exercise 368

Exercise 369

Exercise 370

Exercise 371

Exercise 372

Exercise 373

Exercise 374

Exercise 375

Exercise 376

Exercise 377

Exercise 378

Exercise 379

Exercise 380

Exercise 381

Exercise 382

Exercise 383

Exercise 384

Exercise 385

Exercise 386

Exercise 387

Exercise 388

Exercise 393

Exercise 394

Exercise 395

Exercise 396

Exercise 400

Exercise 401

Exercise 402

Exercise 406

Exercise 407

Exercise 408

Exercise 409

Exercise 410

Exercise 411

Exercise 412

Exercise 413

Exercise 414

Exercise 416

Exercise 417

Exercise 418

Exercise 419

Exercise 420

Exercise 421

Exercise 422

Exercise 423

Exercise 424

Exercise 425

Exercise 426

Exercise 430

Exercise 431

Exercise 432

Exercise 436

Exercise 437

Exercise 438

Exercise 442

Exercise 443

Exercise 444

Exercise 448

Exercise 449

Exercise 450

Exercise 454

Exercise 455

Exercise 456

Exercise 460

Presenting the Hal Leonard JAZZ PLAY-ALONG SERIES

Prices, contents, and availability subject to change without notice.

FOR MORE INFORMATION,
SEE YOUR LOCAL MUSIC DEALER,
OR WRITE TO:

HAL•LEONARD®
CORPORATION
7777 W. BLUEMOUND RD. P.O. BOX 13819
MILWAUKEE, WISCONSIN 53213

Visit Hal Leonard online at
www.halleonard.com
for complete songlists.

0910

The Best-Selling Jazz Book of All Time Is Now Legal!

The Real Books are the most popular jazz books of all time. Since the 1970s, musicians have trusted these volumes to get them through every gig, night after night. The problem is that the books were illegally produced and distributed, without any regard to copyright law, or royalties paid to the composers who created these musical masterpieces.

Hal Leonard is very proud to present the first legitimate and legal editions of these books ever produced. You won't even notice the difference, other than all the notorious errors being fixed: the covers and typeface look the same, the song lists are nearly identical, and the price for our edition is even cheaper than the originals!

Every conscientious musician will appreciate that these books are now produced accurately and ethically, benefitting the songwriters that we owe for some of the greatest tunes of all time!

VOLUME 1
00240221	C Edition	$39.99
00240224	B♭ Edition	$39.99
00240225	E♭ Edition	$39.99
00240226	Bass Clef Edition	$39.99
00286389	F Edition	$39.99
00240292	C Edition 6 x 9	$35.00
00240339	B♭ Edition 6 x 9	$35.00
00147792	Bass Clef Edition 6 x 9	$35.00
00451087	C Edition on CD-ROM	$29.99
00200984	Online Backing Tracks: Selections	$45.00
00110604	Book/USB Flash Drive Backing Tracks Pack	$79.99
00110599	USB Flash Drive Only	$50.00

VOLUME 2
00240222	C Edition	$39.99
00240227	B♭ Edition	$39.99
00240228	E♭ Edition	$39.99
00240229	Bass Clef Edition	$39.99
00240293	C Edition 6 x 9	$35.00
00125900	B♭ Edition 6 x 9	$35.00
00451088	C Edition on CD-ROM	$30.99
00125900	The Real Book – Mini Edition	$35.00
00204126	Backing Tracks on USB Flash Drive	$50.00
00204131	C Edition – USB Flash Drive Pack	$79.99

VOLUME 3
00240233	C Edition	$39.99
00240284	B♭ Edition	$39.99
00240285	E♭ Edition	$39.99
00240286	Bass Clef Edition	$39.99
00240338	C Edition 6 x 9	$35.00
00451089	C Edition on CD-ROM	$29.99

VOLUME 4
00240296	C Edition	$39.99
00103348	B♭ Edition	$39.99
00103349	E♭ Edition	$39.99
00103350	Bass Clef Edition	$39.99

VOLUME 5
00240349	C Edition	$39.99
00175278	B♭ Edition	$39.99
00175279	E♭ Edition	$39.99

VOLUME 6
00240534	C Edition	$39.99
00223637	E♭ Edition	$39.99

Also available:
00154230	The Real Bebop Book	$34.99
00240264	The Real Blues Book	$34.99
00310910	The Real Bluegrass Book	$35.00
00240223	The Real Broadway Book	$35.00
00240440	The Trane Book	$22.99
00125426	The Real Country Book	$39.99
00269721	The Real Miles Davis Book C Edition	$24.99
00269723	The Real Miles Davis Book B♭ Edition	$24.99
00240355	The Real Dixieland Book C Edition	$32.50
00294853	The Real Dixieland Book E♭ Edition	$35.00
00122335	The Real Dixieland Book B♭ Edition	$35.00
00240235	The Duke Ellington Real Book	$22.99
00240268	The Real Jazz Solos Book	$30.00
00240348	The Real Latin Book C Edition	$37.50
00127107	The Real Latin Book B♭ Edition	$35.00
00120809	The Pat Metheny Real Book C Edition	$27.50
00252119	The Pat Metheny Real Book B♭ Edition	$24.99
00240358	The Charlie Parker Real Book C Edition	$19.99
00275997	The Charlie Parker Real Book E♭ Edition	$19.99
00118324	The Real Pop Book – Vol. 1	$35.00
00240331	The Bud Powell Real Book	$19.99
00240437	The Real R&B Book C Edition	$39.99
00276590	The Real R&B Book B♭ Edition	$39.99
00240313	The Real Rock Book	$35.00
00240323	The Real Rock Book – Vol. 2	$35.00
00240359	The Real Tab Book	$32.50
00240317	The Real Worship Book	$29.99

THE REAL CHRISTMAS BOOK
00240306	C Edition	$32.50
00240345	B♭ Edition	$32.50
00240346	E♭ Edition	$35.00
00240347	Bass Clef Edition	$32.50
00240431	A-G CD Backing Tracks	$24.99
00240432	H-M CD Backing Tracks	$24.99
00240433	N-Y CD Backing Tracks	$24.99

THE REAL VOCAL BOOK
00240230	Volume 1 High Voice	$35.00
00240307	Volume 1 Low Voice	$35.00
00240231	Volume 2 High Voice	$35.00
00240308	Volume 2 Low Voice	$35.00
00240391	Volume 3 High Voice	$35.00
00240392	Volume 3 Low Voice	$35.00
00118318	Volume 4 High Voice	$35.00
00118319	Volume 4 Low Voice	$35.00

Complete song lists online at www.halleonard.com

0719
318